"BARMBY MOOR C.E.
SCHOOL PROPERTY.
PLEASE RETURN THIS BOOK
AS SOON AS POSSIBLE"

OXFORD
First Encyclopedia
Science
and
Technology

Andrew Langley

OXFORD UNIVERSITY PRESS

Oxford University Press,
Great Clarendon Street,
Oxford OX2 6DP

Oxford New York Athens Auckland Bangkok
Bogotá Buenos Aires Calcutta Cape Town Chennai
Dar es Salaam Delhi Florence Hong Kong Istanbul
Karachi Kuala Lumpur Madrid Melbourne Mexico
City Mumbai Nairobi Paris São Paulo Singapore
Taipei Tokyo Toronto Warsaw and associated
companies in Berlin Ibadan

Oxford is a registered trade mark of
Oxford University Press

© Andrew Langley 1999

All rights reserved. No part of this publication may
be reproduced, stored in a retrieval system, or
transmitted, in any form or by any means, without
the prior permission in writing of Oxford
University Press. Within the UK, exceptions are
allowed in respect of any fair dealing for the
purpose of research or private study, or criticism or
review, as permitted under the Copyright, Designs
and Patents Act 1988, or in the case of reprographic
reproduction in accordance with the terms of the
licences issued by the Copyright Licensing Agency.
Enquiries concerning reproduction outside these
terms and in other countries should be sent to the
Rights Department, Oxford University Press, at the
address above

This book is sold subject to the condition that it
shall not, by way of trade or otherwise, be lent, re-
sold, hired out or otherwise circulated without the
publisher's prior consent in any form of binding or
cover other than that in which it is published and
without a similar condition including this
condition being imposed on the subsequent
purchaser

British Library Cataloguing in
Publication Data
Data available

ISBN 0–19–910559–6 (hardback)
ISBN 0–19–910560–X (paperback)
1–3–5–7–9–10–8–6–4–2

Printed in Portugal by Edições ASA

Contents

Science and Technology

The word "science" means knowledge. Science helps us to understand how the world is made, and how it works. Scientists ask questions about the world, then try to find answers using tests called experiments. All the time, scientists are discovering wonderful new things about our world. We use their discoveries to make our lives safer and easier. We have fires and fuels to keep us warm. We have machines of all kinds, and medicines to cure disease. The many ways of using science are what we call technology.

What is everything made of?

Everything in the world is made of something. This "something" is called matter. You are made of matter – and so is everything else, from mountains to ice creams. Even the air you breathe is made of matter. All this matter comes in one of three states – as a solid, as a liquid or as a gas.

The three states

The waterfall, the rocks and the wind moving the clouds in this picture are all very different kinds of matter. The rock is hard, and has a fixed shape. We call it a solid. The waterfall is made of water, and has no fixed shape. It is a liquid. The wind is made of air, which is a gas. A gas will fill any space it is put into.

Changing states

Matter does not always stay the same. It can change from one state to another. A solid can become a liquid, and a liquid can become a gas. It is easy to see these changes with water.

Ice is solid water. If you heat a piece of ice, it melts and turns into a liquid.

If you heat the water more, it boils and turns into steam. The steam is a gas.

heat

steam (gas)

ice cube (solid)

water (liquid)

Changing shapes

We can make many useful objects by heating materials to melt them, then changing their shape before they cool down again. Metals such as iron or gold are solid, but when they are heated a lot they melt and become liquids. This hot liquid is poured into shaped moulds. When it cools down, it becomes a solid in the shape of the mould.

Frying tonight

Heating a liquid can turn it into a solid! The next time you have fried eggs, watch them being cooked. The egg is runny when it goes into the pan, but as it gets hot, it turns solid. This is a different sort of change from when something melts, because the egg stays solid when it cools down.

◁ These workers are pouring very hot metal into moulds. Their silver suits and special visors (masks) help to protect them from the heat.

Building blocks

We know that everything is made of matter. But what is matter made of? Imagine that you could chop an iron bar into little pieces. Then imagine chopping one of those pieces into even tinier bits. If you kept cutting the smaller and smaller pieces, eventually you would have the tiniest bits of all. These are called atoms. All matter is made from atoms.

◁ This part of the salt grain has been magnified even further, to show the atoms. There are two sorts in salt – sodium and chlorine.

Millions of atoms

A pile of salt contains millions of tiny grains of salt. It is easy to see one salt grain, but just one of these grains contains millions of atoms. The atoms are so tiny that you cannot see them.

△ The oblong shapes in this photograph are grains of salt. The photo has been made many times bigger to help you see the grains more clearly. Even so, the salt atoms are too small to see.

▽ Each of these building blocks has the name of an element on it.

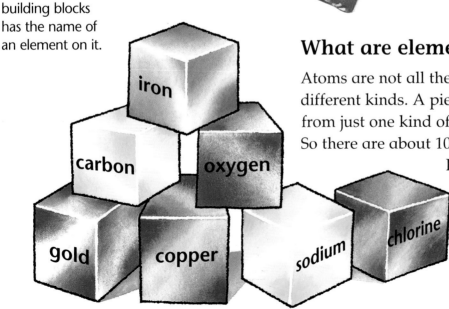

What are elements?

Atoms are not all the same. There are about 100 different kinds. A piece of matter which is made from just one kind of atom is called an element. So there are about 100 different elements.

Elements are the "building blocks" for all other kinds of matter. They can be put together in different ways to make millions of kinds of matter.

iron

carbon   oxygen

gold   copper   sodium   chlorine

How we use matter

Matter comes in many different forms. It can be hard or soft, heavy or light. You can see through some kinds of matter (like air), but not through others (like coal). A bicycle contains lots of different kinds of matter. Each one has a special use for the rider.

 ## Amazing atoms

More than a million atoms would fit on to the thickness of one human hair!

this plastic is tough and light

this plastic is flexible and waterproof

cotton is soft but keeps in the warmth

The hardest

Diamonds are the hardest material in the world. Scientists are trying to make a new kind of glass with a diamond coating. This glass will be so hard that you could never scratch it.

glass is clear

△ These diamonds are on a piece of kimberlite, which is the rock that diamonds are found in.

metal is strong

rubber is soft and bendy

Making materials

Everything around us is made of materials. We can use some materials, such as wood or stone, without changing them very much. But we can also change materials into something very different. We can turn trees into paper, or oil into plastic, or sand into glass. Each of these materials has a different job to do.

tree

wood chips

pulp

Wool

Wool is a warm and tough material. It grows as a hairy coat called a fleece on sheep, goats and other animals. The fleece is cut off the animal and washed. The tangled fibres of wool are combed straight, then twisted together to make a long thread. This twisting is known as spinning. The wool thread can be woven or knitted to make clothes.

sheep

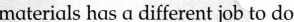

fleece

combing

pulling

spinning

ball of wool

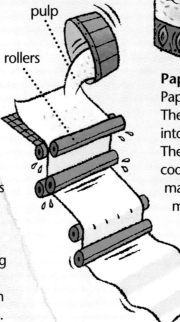

pulp

rollers

paper

Paper

Paper is made from wood. The wood from trees is cut into small pieces, or chips. These wood chips are then cooked with chemicals to make the fibres soft. This mixture of cooked wood chips is called pulp. The soggy pulp is laid out and rolled flat. When it is dry, the fibres grow hard again. They stick together to form paper.

Something new

To make a new material, you have to start with natural substances. These are called the raw materials. Trees are the raw materials for paper. Rocks are the raw materials for metal. The raw materials are taken to a factory, where they are changed into new materials.

paper

plastic

steel

wool

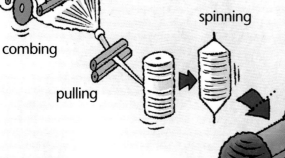

Iron and steel

Iron is found mixed up with other chemicals in a rock called iron ore. The iron ore is broken up and heated in a huge oven called a blast furnace. The iron part of the ore melts and runs out of the furnace. To make steel from iron, another furnace is used. Steel is much stronger than iron.

iron ore

melted iron

blast furnace

steel furnace

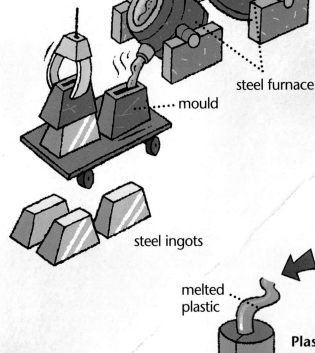

mould

steel ingots

melted plastic

mould

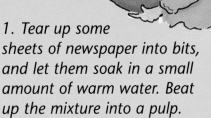

oil

Plastic

Plastic is light and easy to bend into different shapes. It is made from oil found under the ground. The oil is treated with chemicals to make plastic. When the plastic is heated, it melts into a thick liquid. This can be squashed or moulded into thousands of different shapes.

finished bottles

New paper from old

Here is a way to turn old newspapers into your own recycled paper.

1. Tear up some sheets of newspaper into bits, and let them soak in a small amount of warm water. Beat up the mixture into a pulp.

2. Tip the pulp onto a piece of blotting paper or a tea towel, and spread it out into an even sheet.

3. Put more blotting paper or another tea towel over the pulp. Roll it with a rolling pin, then ask a grown-up to iron it. When dry, carefully peel off the blotting paper or tea towels. There is your recycled paper!

Strong structures

Have you ever been to the top of a tall building? Or travelled through a long, deep tunnel? Or crossed a bridge over a wide valley? Perhaps you wondered how these huge structures were made – and how they stay up! Skyscrapers, tunnels and bridges need to be made of strong materials, like concrete and steel, and they need clever engineers who can make sure that the structures are safe.

Going up . . .

Some skyscrapers are so tall that they sway in the wind. They must be built so that they can bend, but will not break. Steel and concrete are sunk into the earth to make a steady base for the building. A strong column of concrete is built in the centre of the skyscraper. Then a framework of steel is attached to the column, to hold the floors. The outside of this frame is covered with panels made of light metal and glass.

central core with lifts

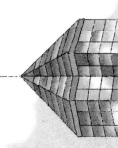

steel frame

Ancient builders

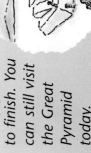

Long ago, people did not have strong machines or tools. But they could still make amazing structures. About 100,000 workers built the Great Pyramid in Egypt, using over 2 million huge blocks of stone. Even so, it took many years to finish. You can still visit the Great Pyramid today.

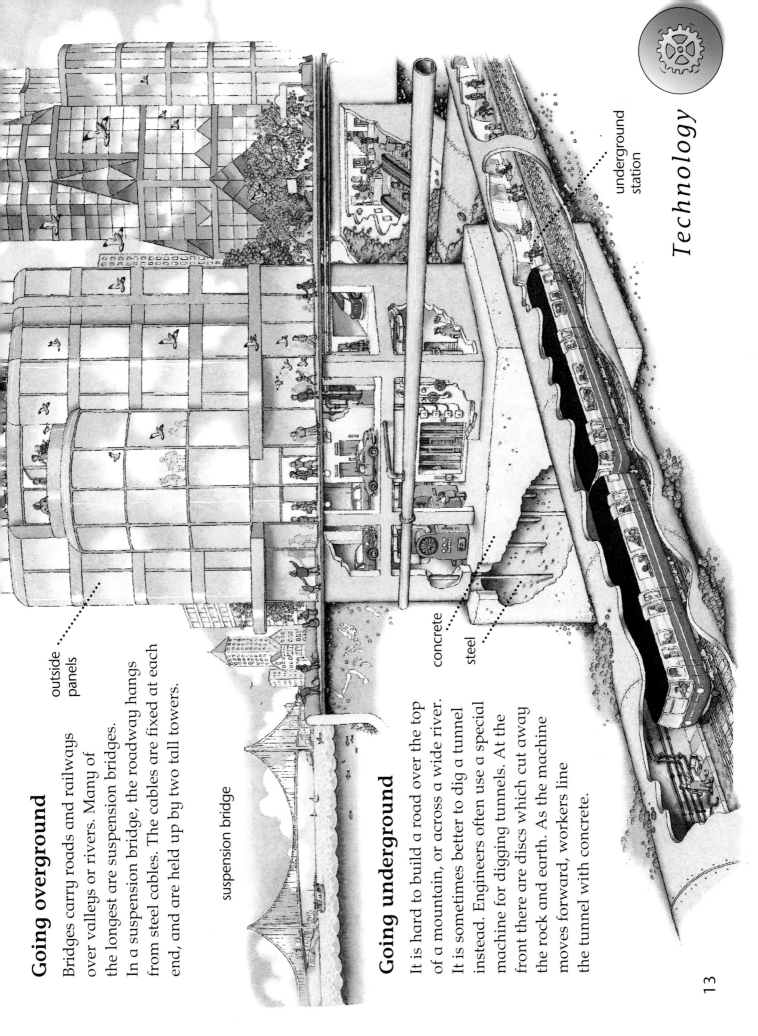

Going overground

Bridges carry roads and railways over valleys or rivers. Many of the longest are suspension bridges. In a suspension bridge, the roadway hangs from steel cables. The cables are fixed at each end, and are held up by two tall towers.

outside panels

suspension bridge

Going underground

It is hard to build a road over the top of a mountain, or across a wide river. It is sometimes better to dig a tunnel instead. Engineers often use a special machine for digging tunnels. At the front there are discs which cut away the rock and earth. As the machine moves forward, workers line the tunnel with concrete.

concrete

steel

underground station

Everything needs energy

You need energy to keep you going. Without it, your body cannot walk, run, breathe or even think! You get your energy from food. Other things need energy to keep going, too. Animals get energy from food, like us. Plants get their energy from the Sun. A car gets energy from petrol. A television gets energy from electricity. A sailing ship gets energy from the wind.

Making things happen

There are many different sources of energy, even around your home. You cannot always see where the energy is coming from. Anything that moves or changes is using energy from somewhere.

sunlight helps the plants to grow

petrol makes the car work

electricity makes the lawn mower work

heat from burning coal cooks the food

food gives you the energy to run and play

Storing energy

Energy from the Sun can be stored away and used later. One of these stored sources of energy is oil. It is made from tiny plants and animals that were squashed together over millions of years. Petrol and other fuels come from oil. So cars, lorries, aircraft and ships all use energy from very old animals and plants!

wind keeps the kite in the air and dries the wet clothes

! **Pedal power**

The energy from one litre of petrol will drive a car about 16 kilometres. If you use the same amount of energy on a bicycle, you could cycle over 500 kilometres!

The energy factory

Where does energy come from? Most of it starts in one place – the Sun. Heat and light from the Sun travel through space to the Earth. Grass and other plants use the Sun's energy to grow. Then cows and other animals eat the grass. Cows turn some of the energy from the grass into milk. If you drink the milk, the energy passes into your body.

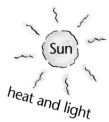

Sun

heat and light

grass

milk

Pushing and pulling

All around you, things are being pushed or pulled. When you kick a ball, you are pushing it. When a crane lifts a heavy load, it pulls it into the air. Pushes and pulls are forces. Forces can make objects speed up, slow down or change the direction they move in.

Body force

You can use the muscles in your body to produce a force. When you pick up a spoon, the muscles in your arm pull on the bones to make the arm bend. Weightlifters have very strong muscles. They can pick up much heavier things than spoons!

▽ As the weightlifter begins to lift, he pulls on the bar to get it off the floor.

▷ Once he has got the weights to his chest, the weightlifter gives a huge push to lift the bar above his head.

! *Big lift*
Andrey Chermenkin of Russia lifted a world record 260 kilograms in a weightlifting contest in 1996. This is like lifting almost four full-grown men above your head at the same time!

The pull of gravity

If you drop a stone, it falls to the ground. A special force is pulling the stone downwards, towards the centre of the Earth. We call this force gravity. Everything on Earth is pulled down by gravity. Even when you stand still, the gravity of the Earth is pulling you downwards. Without it you would float in the air!

The force of friction

If you sit down on a grassy slope, you won't slide down it. This is because a force called friction stops you. The surface of your clothes and the grass are both rough. They catch on each other, and stop you from moving. A slide has a much smoother surface than grass. The force of friction is much less here, so you slide easily.

▽ Ice is good for sliding, too, because it is very smooth. If you wear ice skates, you can slide even faster. Wheee!

Fun with magnets

Have you ever played with a magnet? It contains a special kind of force – magnetic force. A magnet attracts many metal objects. It will pick up things like paper clips and nails.

A magnet has two ends, or poles, called north and south. You can see for yourself, if you have two magnets.

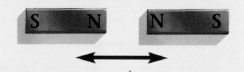

Place the two north poles of the magnets together. They will push away from each other. The two south poles together do the same.

But if you put a north pole with a south pole, the magnets attract each other.

The needle of a compass is a magnet. It always points north because the Earth is a magnet, too – a very big one!

17

Machines in action

We use machines every day. They help us do an amazing number of things. At home, they clean the clothes, make the toast, play music, wash the dishes and mow the lawn. Big machines like cars and trains carry us from place to place. Even bigger machines help to build buildings and roads. In factories, machines help to make everything from plastic toys to aircraft.

! Super ship

Oil tankers are probably the biggest machines ever made. Some of these ships are so long that they have room for five football pitches on deck!

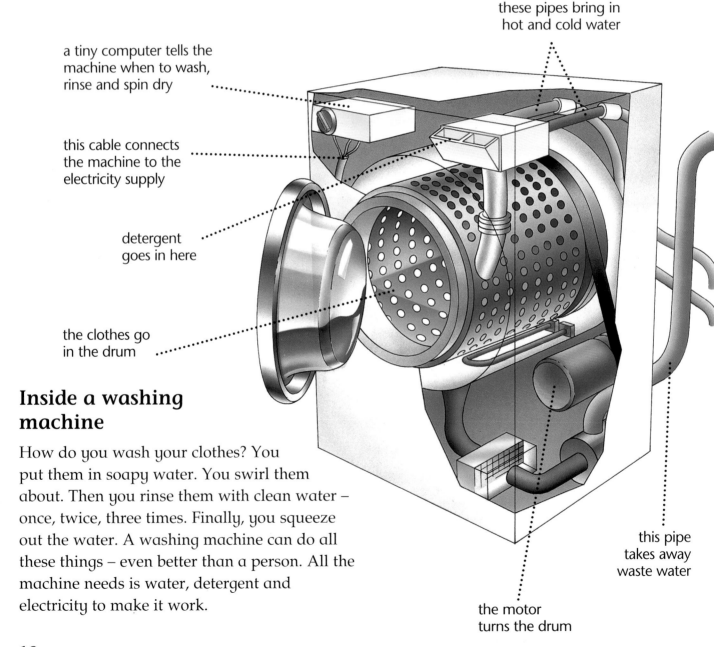

these pipes bring in hot and cold water

a tiny computer tells the machine when to wash, rinse and spin dry

this cable connects the machine to the electricity supply

detergent goes in here

the clothes go in the drum

this pipe takes away waste water

the motor turns the drum

Inside a washing machine

How do you wash your clothes? You put them in soapy water. You swirl them about. Then you rinse them with clean water – once, twice, three times. Finally, you squeeze out the water. A washing machine can do all these things – even better than a person. All the machine needs is water, detergent and electricity to make it work.

Robot worker

Some machines can work
by themselves. We call them
robots. Every move they make
is controlled by a computer.
In car factories, robots help to
put cars together. They do the
more dangerous jobs, such
as welding (joining pieces
of metal by heating them)
and spraying paint.

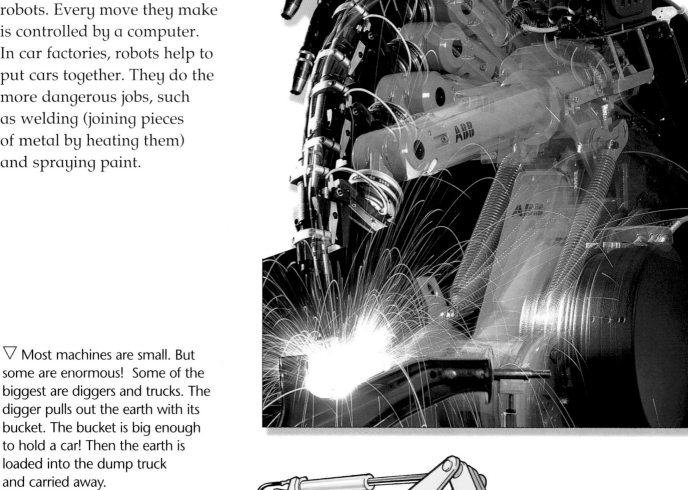

▽ Most machines are small. But
some are enormous! Some of the
biggest are diggers and trucks. The
digger pulls out the earth with its
bucket. The bucket is big enough
to hold a car! Then the earth is
loaded into the dump truck
and carried away.

19

Light and sound

What happens when you wake up in the morning? Perhaps you see the sunlight through your bedroom window? Perhaps you hear the sound of the alarm clock beside your bed? Different lights and sounds are around us all through the day.

Light and dark

What can you see in the dark? Of course, you cannot see anything. You need light to see things. Light is a kind of energy. It can travel freely through the air. The Sun gives us light in the daytime. At night, we get light from electric lamps, torches and candles.

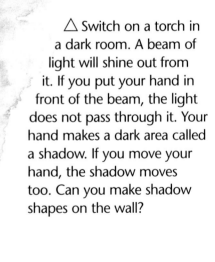

△ Switch on a torch in a dark room. A beam of light will shine out from it. If you put your hand in front of the beam, the light does not pass through it. Your hand makes a dark area called a shadow. If you move your hand, the shadow moves too. Can you make shadow shapes on the wall?

◁ When the light from your torch reaches something shiny, it bounces back, or reflects. This is why you can see yourself in a mirror. A mirror is very smooth and shiny. When light from your face reaches the mirror, the light bounces straight back, and you see a picture of yourself.

Sounds all around

Listen! What sounds can you hear? If you are in a very noisy place, you may hear loud sounds, like the roar of an aircraft or the rat-a-tat of a road drill. If you are in a quiet place, you may hear the ticking of a clock or the buzzing of a fly. So what are sounds? And how are they made?

Making sounds

Put your hand against your throat. Now hum loudly. You will feel your throat shaking, or vibrating. The vibrations come from the voice box inside your throat. All sounds are made by vibrations like these. A drum vibrates when you hit it. These vibrations make the air around vibrate too. The vibrations in the air are sound waves. They spread out like waves in water.

▷ Sound waves can bounce back – just like beams of light. What happens if you stand in a big empty room and shout? A moment later, you hear your shout again. This is an echo of your voice. The echo is the sound waves from your voice bouncing off the ceiling or walls.

Electricity

Imagine a world without electricity. You would have no television, no freezer, no vacuum cleaner, no electric cooker and no electric light. There would be no telephones and no computers. All of these things are powered by electricity. Electricity is one of the most important kinds of energy in the world.

Power at home

We use electricity in many ways at home. Electricity can make things work, like the washing machine or the food mixer. It can produce light in a light bulb. It can also produce heat, in an electric cooker or a toaster.

▽ A large city at night is a blaze of light. The power for all these lights comes from electricity.

Safety first

Beware! Electricity can be very dangerous. If you touch a bare wire you can get an electric shock. So, NEVER touch electric sockets or plugs. Always ask a grown-up to help you.

▷ Electric wires are made of metals like copper, because electricity flows easily through them. Electricity cannot flow through plastic, so the wires are usually covered with plastic.

Electricity goes round

The bulb is not lit. When you connect it with a wire to a battery, the bulb lights up! There is electrical energy inside the battery. This energy flows along the wire to the bulb. Electrical energy will only light the bulb if it is connected in a circle back to the battery. The circle is called a circuit.

copper wire

plastic cover

the bulb lights up when electricity flows through it

the switch lets you turn the flow of electricity on and off.

electricity travels along the wire

electricity is made in the battery

Power station

Most of the electricity we use comes from huge buildings called power stations. Here, coal, oil or gas is burned to heat water and make steam. The steam turns giant machines which make electricity flow. This electricity travels along thick wires to factories, shops, schools and homes.

Talking to each other

When you are sitting at home, it is easy to pick up the telephone and talk to a friend far away. You can switch on the television and watch a game of basketball in a foreign country. You can turn on the radio and hear music. Telephones, televisions and radios can bring messages into your home from all over the world.

satellite

Sending signals

Everyone wants to watch the Olympic Games. They are watched on television by millions of people – all at the same time. Television engineers send signals from television cameras all round the world in an instant.

◁ The satellite dish turns the electric signals into radio signals, and sends them to a satellite high above the Earth.

satellite dish

▷ First, the pictures of the runners have to be changed into electric signals. The camera does this. The signals travel down a wire to a satellite dish.

electric signals

camera

Waves through the air

▽ The satellite passes on the radio signals to another satellite dish on a TV station on the other side of the world. A transmitter sends them on to your TV at home.

The signals that reach your radio or television do not travel along wires all the way to your home. They travel part of the way through the air, just like waves of sound. They are called radio signals. Thousands and sometimes millions of these signals reach your radio every second.

television station

transmitter

On the phone

You cannot talk to a radio or a television, but a telephone is different. It sends messages both ways – out from your home, and in from the people who phone you. When you speak into the mouthpiece of a telephone, your words are turned into an electric signal. The signal travels down the wire to your friend. The voice of your friend travels back to you in just the same way.

Cardboard TV

The very first television set was made by a man called John Logie Baird in 1924. He used all sorts of things to build it. These included sheets of cardboard, knitting needles, a biscuit tin and sealing wax!

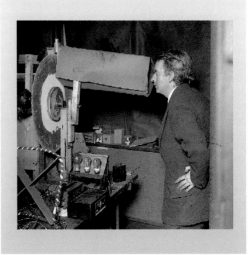

TV set

△ Your television changes the signals back into pictures and sounds.

Computers

We build most machines to do one special job. An electric drill makes holes. A hairdryer dries your hair. A clock tells you the time. But a computer can do lots of jobs. It can do sums and it can store information. It can help you to write letters and to draw plans. It does all these things using tiny electronic circuits called "microchips".

Computers at work

We tell a computer what to do by typing on the keyboard or by clicking the mouse. The computer can do what we ask because it has a set of instructions called a program stored on microchips inside it. There are many kinds of program, and each one has a different set of instructions.

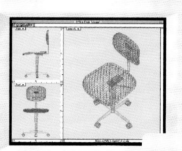

▽ Some programs work with words and numbers. Banks, shops and office workers use these programs.

△ Other programs work with drawings and plans. Engineers and designers use these programs.

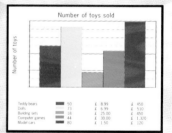

△ Computer games are another kind of program. You might have some on a computer at home or at school.

Hidden computers

Lots of the things that we use every day have a computer inside them. This is a computer, even though it does not look like one! Inside this video camera is a tiny computer, which controls the way the camera works.

Books on chips

Computers can store enormous amounts of information on one tiny microchip. All the words and pictures in this encyclopedia can be stored on a chip the same size as your fingertip!

Glossary

atoms tiny particles that make up everything around us.

battery a source of electricity that is portable.

concrete a mixture of water, sand, cement and gravel, which sets hard to make a strong material for building.

detergent a cleaning substance that helps to lift dirt and grease off things that need cleaning.

element a material that is made of only one kind of atom. Metals such as iron and gold are elements.

engineer a person who works out how to build bridges, machines and buildings.

fibres thin strands or threads. Cotton and wool are materials made from fibres.

force a push or a pull.

friction a force caused by things rubbing together.

fuel something which is used up to produce energy, for example by burning it.

gravity the force that pulls objects towards the Earth.

material anything used for making something else. Wood, paper, plastic, cotton and metals are all common materials.

microchip a tiny electronic circuit, no bigger than a fingernail. Microchips are used in computers, videos and other electronic equipment.

mineral a type of substance found in the ground, such as oil or coal.

mould a hollow shape into which a liquid is poured. The liquid then sets in the shape of the mould.

muscle a bundle of fibres that tightens or relaxes to move part of the body.

ore a rock which is rich in one type of metal.

program a set of instructions for a computer that tell it how to do a particular job.

recycled paper paper made from other paper, rather than from trees.

satellite a moon or a spacecraft that circles around a planet.

signal a changing electric current or radio wave that carries information.

skyscraper a building so tall that it seems to "scrape the sky".

structure a bulding, a bridge, a tower, or anything else that has been built.

transmitter a piece of electronic equipment that sends out radio or television signals.

Index

A

air   6, 9
atom   8–9

B

battery   23
bicycle   9, 15
blast furnace   11
bones   16
bridge   12–13
building   12–13

C

car   14, 18
carbon   8
chlorine   8
circuit   23, 26
coal   9, 14, 23
compass   17
computer   18, 19, 22, 26
concrete   12–13
copper   8, 23
cotton   9
cow   15
crane   16

D

dark   20
day   20
diamond   9
digger   19

E

Earth   17
echo   21
Egypt   12
electricity   14, 18, 20, 22–23, 24–25
element   8
energy   14–15, 20–23
engineer   12–13, 24, 26

F

food   14–15
friction   17

G

gas   6–7, 23
glass   9, 10, 12
goat   10
gold   7, 8
grass   15
gravity   17

H

heat   22

I

ice   6, 17
iron   7, 8, 11

K

kimberlite   9
kite   15
knitting   11

L

light   20, 22, 23
liquid   6–7

M

machine   5, 18–19
magnet   17
matter   6–9
medicine   5
metal   7, 9, 11, 23
microchip   26
milk   15
mirror   20
mould   11
muscles   16

N

night   20
North Pole   17

O

oil   15, 23, 10–11
oil tanker   18
ore   11
oxygen   8

P

paper   10–11
petrol   14–15
plants   14–15
plastic   9, 23, 10–11
power station   23
pyramid   12

Acknowledgements

Abbreviations: t = top; b = bottom; c = centre; l = left; r = right; (back) = background; (fore) = foreground.

Illustrations
Cover Science Photo Library; cover tr Oxford illustrators; back cover tl Georgie Birkett; 5 Clive Goodyer; 6bc, br Scot Ritchie; 7tr Scot Ritchie; 8bl Clive Goodyer; 8tr Joshua Smith; 9l Lynne Willey; 10br Lynne Willey; 10l, r Clive Goodyer; 11r Scot Ritchie; 11r Clive Goodyer; 12b Scot Ritchie; 12–13 Benedict Blaythwayt; 14–15 Annabel Spenceley; 15tr Scot Ritchie; 15cr Clive Goodyer; 17bl, t Scot Ritchie; 117cr Tessa Eccles; 17br Alan Fred Pipes; 18t Scot Ritchie; 18b Oxford Illustrators; 19b Andy Burton; 20t Lynne Willey; 20b Scot Ritchie; 21tl Lynne Willey; 21tr Clive Goodyer; 21b Scot Ritchie; 22tr Clive Goodyer; 23t Clive Goodyer; 24b Doug Gray; 24–25 Clive Goodyer; 25cr Doug Gray; 25b Clive Goodyear; 26cl, c, cr Joshua Smith; 26br Scot Ritchie.

Photographs
The publishers would like to thank the following for permission to reproduce photographs:
6t Natural History Photo Archive (NHPA); 7b Science Photo Library; 8c Science Photo Library; 9r De Beers; 16 Action Plus; 19t Science Photo Library; 22b Robert Harding; 23b Science Photo Library; 25tr Getty Images; 26bl Sony.